THE FAR SIDE Gallery 5

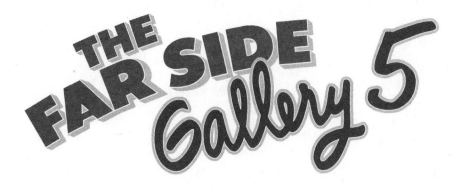

Other Books in The Far Side Series

The Far Side
Beyond The Far Side
In Search of The Far Side
Bride of The Far Side
Valley of The Far Side
It Came From The Far Side
Hound of The Far Side
The Far Side Observer
Night of the Crash-Test Dummies
Wildlife Preserves
Wiener Dog Art
Unnatural Selections
Cows of Our Planet
The Chickens Are Restless
The Curse of Madame "C"

Anthologies

The Far Side Gallery
The Far Side Gallery 2
The Far Side Gallery 3
The Far Side Gallery 4

Retrospective

The PreHistory of The Far Side: A 10th Anniversary Exhibit

THE FAR SIDE Gallery 5

By
GARY LARSON

Andrews and McMeel
A Universal Press Syndicate Company
Kansas City

Library of Congress Catalog Card Number: 95-77571

ISBN: 0-8362-1306-8

Foreword

In 1988 Gary Larson went on safari to Africa and one of the places he visited was the Gombe National Park in Tanzania, home of the chimpanzees made famous by the *National Geographic* magazines and documentaries. As we sat around the fire the first evening, Gary told me he had been quite apprehensive about our meeting—because of the "Jane Goodall Tramp" cartoon. That story has already been told—from his side—by Gary. But nobody has told my side. I was in Tanzania when the infamous cartoon first appeared. So I knew nothing about the minicommotion that went on at the time until I went to America for a lecture tour. When I got to the Jane Goodall Institute office, my *then* executive director thrust the cartoon at me. "Just look at that, will you!" she announced, in icy tones. I thought the folded paper must contain some bad news so I opened it apprehensively. When I saw it I remember making some kind of explosive mirthful sound—I like to think it was a guffaw, because that is such a wonderful word, a real *Far Side* sort of word. And I said something like: "Wow! Fantastic! Real fame at last! Fancy being in a Gary Larson cartoon!" I could hardly believe it when the *then* executive director told me she had found it so offensive that she had asked a lawyer to write a letter of complaint! It implied, she said, that I had sexual relations with the chimps!! I thought she was joking, until I saw her closed and silent face. And she showed me the letter, which had appeared in the local newspaper.

I was so angry that I intended to write Gary Larson myself, to apologize, but I got whirled into the frenzy of the tour—and I forgot. So the next thing, a year or so later, was an urgent call from the National Geographic Society. They wanted to reproduce the Jane Goodall Tramp cartoon in their centennial volume but Larson's company had refused permission—they were afraid that my institute would sue them! I remember frantic transatlantic phone calls between the Geographic, Larson's attorney, my Institute (with quite a different director!), and myself. In the end I had to go to a notary and declare, under oath, that I had no intention of bringing a lawsuit against Gary Larson, or his company, ever! Eventually the JGI benefited enormously because Gary gave us permission to put the cartoon on a T-shirt and it is one of

"Well, well—another blond hair. … Conducting a little more 'research' with that Jane Goodall tramp?"

our hottest numbers! The only real problem it has given me is the sheer number of copies of the thing that people have sent me—and I never like to throw them away. I have enough now to paper a small room. The trouble is, there is only one room small enough—and that doesn't seem quite polite!

When I tell people that Gary Larson has been to Gombe they are first impressed, then curious. What is he really like, as a person? Does he go around making Far Side jokes? Does he have a bizarre sense of humor? I found him utterly delightful, quiet, and very observant. He has a wonderfully kind sense of humor. I never heard him talking Larsonesque Far Side language in public! He was interested, as one would expect, in everything around him. I remember that Gary spent hours, with his video, stalking the brilliant butterflies of the Gombe forests.

He and his wife had decided to sleep in a small tent (the rest of their little group, which included Jack Lemmon, had opted for rooms in my house or the guest house). They had all arrived late in the afternoon and as we walked along the beach of Lake Tanganyika to look for a good place for the tent, the sun was already low over the Zaire hills in the west. Gary and his wife refused all offers of help, so we left them to sort out the tent themselves. The rest of us had a refreshing swim, then gathered on the beach outside my house for a drink. We sat there, listening to the little waves flipping over onto the shore, enjoying the glow of the setting sun on the moving water. It sank behind the western hills. Slowly the sunset faded. Our glasses were empty. And still they had not joined us. We presumed they were just enjoying the solitude—but when they eventually appeared it turned out that they had been struggling with the vagaries of the tent all that time, desperately trying to transform the little bundle of canvas and metal rods into something that looked roughly like a place where they could spend the night! And I don't think they made that good a job of it even then—I seem to remember that the whole thing collapsed the next morning under the small weight of young baboons sliding playfully down the canvas!

One incident stands out vividly in my memory. As Gary and I were walking back through the forest one evening, we encountered Frodo, grandson of the famous chimpanzee matriarch, Flo. Frodo the bully. He has always been a bully, always loved to intimidate any individual, chimpanzee or human, weaker than himself. And even in those days, when he was merely a rambunctious adolescent, he was already stronger than Gary and I put together. I knew we were in trouble when he changed course and made a beeline for us. "Hang onto a tree!" I told Gary. As Frodo pulled and pushed and hit my illustrious visitor, I remained outwardly calm. Actually I was terrified—there I was, responsible for the safety of one of the most talented cartoonists of all time, and there was Frodo trying to throw Gary Larson to the ground! Usually I was the target of Frodo's unpleasant bullying, but on that occasion, even though I tried (for the only time in my life!) to divert Frodo's attentions to myself, he was only interested in Gary. Of course, Frodo wasn't really trying to hurt, just "playfully" trying to intimidate, and luckily he eventually gave up and left us in peace.

Gary visited Gombe during his "sabbatical." Soon thereafter he went back to work and produced another five years' worth of fantastic Far Side cartoons. Gary's humor has infiltrated twentieth-century culture. His cows and deer, his

sharks and snakes and insects, along with the strange lantern-jawed small-headed humans, are everywhere. Pinned to college notice boards, stuck on the outside—and the inside—of people's doors, on the walls. All over North America, all over Europe and many other parts of the world. The Far Side cartoons in the newspapers guaranteed readers the opportunity to start their day with a smile, a chuckle—or even a guffaw! Some of Gary's cartoons, quite simply, are absurd. Like the shipwrecked man struggling toward a little desert island only to see a lone dog under a lone palm tree and a large sign reading "Beware of the Dog." Life's little ironies!

Often Gary's cartoons help us to see things with a new perspective, above all to realize that we humans, after all, are just one species among many, just one small part of the wondrous animal kingdom. Larson blithely reverses the roles of human and nonhuman so that, as you browse through a whole collection you find on one page a Gary Larson human carelessly squishing a foolish dog (yapping when the man of the house is trying to watch the World Cup), and on another, a Gary Larson elephant carelessly squishing a foolish human. Then there is the veterinarian, having completed his examination of a gigantic Larsonesque beetle, who turns to the concerned owner: "I'm sorry, Mr. Caldwell, but the big guy's on his way out. If you want my opinion, take him home, find a quiet spot out in the yard, and squash him." To complete this picture, a normal-sized ant "wearing" a human boot with which he has inadvertently squashed several of his brothers and sisters. "Ernie!" admonishes his mother. "Look what you're doing—take those shoes off!" The whole gamut. Crazy. Absurd. Yet it all helps to put us humans in our place. And we desperately need putting in our place.

Today there is increased awareness about our often thoughtless, sometimes cruel, treatment of nonhuman animals. I believe that The Far Side cartoons have contributed to this growing understanding. The picture of a little old lady sitting on a bench in the park feeding the crocodiles that approach like so many ducks to beg for mice out of a box (with air holes, mind you) or sitting in her living room with a pet octopus on her lap are far out, all right. But such images, collectively, start to make you *think*. Often a particular image stays with you and pops back into your conscious mind later in the day so that you giggle—or guffaw—out loud. It's sort of like eating something delicious that makes you burp, unexpectedly—and probably embarrassingly—some time afterward. So Gary starts us thinking, and then gets us to go on thinking. Hey! There are other critters out there too! They have names and feelings. They matter too. One of my absolute favorites that can make me laugh out loud, even in public, if it suddenly pops into my mind, is the very small head of a very small fly, in the middle of a huge bowl of soup. From the rim another small fly yells desperately, "Barbara, I'm going for help. Tread soup!" I think I especially love cartoons like this because the animals are all *named*. That drowning fly is not just any old fly—she's a fly who matters. She is called Barbara.

How many people have tried to imagine the world from the perspective of a fly? Gary does. There are two terrified little flies walking through "The Fly House of Horrors" gazing, shocked, at the bloated spider sucking a fly's lifeblood, a huge-looking flyswatter, and a Venus's-flytrap. And, of course, as we all know, he sees many things from the perspective of cows. He introduces us to three cows in a car, jabbering out of the window, "Yakity yak yak yak!" as they stare at a field of humans, who are standing, doing nothing. And dog perspectives—a courting dog, with his gift of flowers, effusively greets his date: "Oh, Ginger—you look absolutely stunning … and whatever you rolled in sure does stink."

"I'm sorry, Mr. Caldwell, but the big guy's on his way out. If you want my opinion, take him home, find a quiet spot out in the yard, and squash him."

Recently I was talking with one of the best teachers I know, Tim O'Halloran. He has been able to inspire generations of middle and high school students to care for the natural world. Tim told me that Gary Larson has had a major impact on his teaching. Tim uses Far Side cartoons to introduce topics, to illustrate points, and to "reinforce the notion that the more we investigate the universe, the richer is our experience." When designing exam papers Tim finds the cartoons "ease the tension and spark the memory." It all began when, in the fall of 1985, he was given the task of teaching science to 162 Tulsa ninth-graders who were convinced that it was absolutely irrelevant to their futures. Tim put one hundred Far Side cartoons on a large bulletin board, and told the students to study them. The consensus was that they didn't understand the humor—The Far Side was "too weird." However, Tim wrote me, "Each time we completed a unit and the students approached the bulletin board armed with newly acquired wisdom, I smiled quietly and thanked the cosmos for Gary's perspectives as the kids roared with the confident laughter of the enlightened."

So, how did their knowledge help them? Well, take the cartoon that shows the confrontation of two female mantids on the doorstep, with its caption, "I don't know what you're insinuating, Jane, but I haven't seen your Harold all day—besides, surely you know I would only devour my *own* husband!" This doesn't make sense until you have learned that it is normal practice for a female praying mantis to devour her husband once mating is over (sometimes she starts, on his head, even *before* he has finished). Then there is one captioned, "The last thing that a fly sees," which shows about twelve images of the same large woman with a raised flyswatter. This cannot be appreciated until you know about the compound eyes of flies.

Speakers at scientific conventions often introduce a slide of a Far Side cartoon to illustrate a point, to get a laugh—Far Side humor is often highly appropriate for those involved in science of some sort. Although you don't need to be a scientist to chuckle at the idea of a dog filling himself with water from a garden hose causing his wife to exclaim, "So! Planning on roaming the neighborhood with some of your buddies today?" But it's even funnier when you know how dogs and wolves can mark a huge territory without replenishing their liquid intake. (When Farley Mowat tried to emulate the marking behavior of the wolves he was studying, he simply ran out of juice when he was just one quarter of the way round *their* "neighborhood"!)

But Gary does not only cater to those who know about natural history. He has something for everyone. There are dentist cartoons for the dentists, and doctor cartoons for doctors, and cooking ones for cooks. (I especially love the one where the father is intently reading *The Cold Cereal Cookbook*, yelling at his son, "Oh, wait! Wait, Cory! … Add the cereal *first* and *then* the milk!" Yes, and then *sugar to taste*!) I spend half my life in airplanes these days—and now, every

time the pilot announces turbulence just as the meal service—or, worse, the beverage service—is about to begin, I think of Larson's pilots grinning at each other then swinging the controls from side to side, laughing fit to bust. And Larson often pinpoints the social problems of our time. The dog, pointing a revolver at his bloated master and mistress as they gorge themselves on yet another meal, says, "Hey, bucko … I'm through begging," surely represents the social unrest that lies at the roots of violence in our inner cities.

Gary Larson's genius lies in his ability to combine his astute understanding of human nature, his equally extensive knowledge of natural history, and his extraordinarily well-developed sense of the absurd. There is, for example, the spider, minute on a huge couch, explaining to a bearded psychoanalyst her repetitive nightmare in which her feet get stuck, one by one, to her web. It is a great contribution you have made, Gary. You teach us to poke fun at ourselves, using the most primitive animals to point out the absurdities of our own behavior. Bang on target. I mean—Metamorphosis Nightclubs! Single-cell bars. Amoeba porn films. *Touché*, Mr. Larson, *touché*.

And now Gary Larson is retiring, and we shall miss him. Some of us will miss him very much. But we wish him a wonderful second career. And we can be sure that, as a result of his books, his cartoons will be around for a long time. Thousands more people as yet unborn will be helped to relate to the ironies and the tragedies, the joyfulness and the richness, of life on earth.

Jane Goodall
July 1995

Dedication

Low tides and wetlands always called to my older brother. Armed with nets, jars, flashlights, and an insatiable curiosity, he was always heading off in a quest for creatures of the not-so-deep. And his younger brother (that would be me) would often accompany him on these mostly mucky "expeditions."

I look back now and see that it was my emulation of my brother that spawned my own awe and love of Nature, and I see now, too, that it was largely my brother's sense of humor that shaped my own in those formative years. (It was he, for example, who showed me the beauty and wonder of a jellyfish, and it was he who showed me the beauty and wonder of smacking your sibling in the face with that same jellyfish.)

If I had not had an older brother, or if I had had a *different* older brother, I know that "The Far Side" would have been much, much different. Something like this, I would guess:

Saved by a jellyfish to the head.

In memory of my brother, Dan

"Hey … this could be the chief."

While their owners sleep, nervous little dogs prepare for their day.

The nightly crisis of Todd's stomach vs. Todd's imagination

"And here's the jewel of my collection, purchased for a king's ransom from a one-eyed man in Istanbul. … I give you Zuzu's petals."

"According to these figures, Simmons, your department has lost another No. 2 Double A, and I want you to find it!"

Colonel Sanders at the Pearly Gates

The Blob family at home

"And so please welcome one of this cartoon's most esteemed scientist-like characters, Prof. Boris Needleman, here to present his paper, 'Beyond the Border: Analysis, Statistical Probability, and Speculation of the Existence of Other Cartoons on the Known Comics Page.'"

"You're a long way from Big Poodle, stranger. ... This here is Dead Skunk, and if I were you I'd just keep on movin'."

"Bob! There's a fly on your lip! ... There he goes. ...
He's back! He's back!"

The life and times of Lulu, Mrs. O'Leary's
ill-fated cow

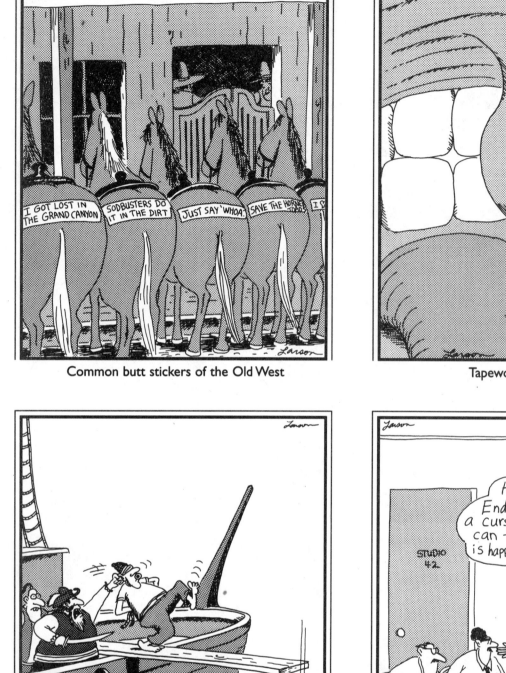

Common butt stickers of the Old West

Tapeworms on vacation

"Whoa whoa whoa, young man!
You *walk* the plank like everyone else!"

The writers for "Bewitched" sit down to their
weekly brainstorming session.

"Care to dance, Ms. Hollings?"

Boid watching

Henry never knew what hit him.

Through mostly grunts and exaggerated gestures,
two fishermen/gatherers attempt to communicate.

"Hey, who's that? ... Oh—Mitch, the janitor. Well, our
first test run has just gotten a little more interesting."

Drive-by erasings

Rhino recitals

Only Bernard, in the front row,
had the nerve to laugh at Death.

Hot off the press, the very first edition of the *Desert
Island Times* caused the newspaper to quickly fold.

"Ha! That finishes it! ... I always knew he'd
be back one day to get the other one!"

"Why don't you play some blues, Andrew?"

Social morays

Suddenly, Fish and Wildlife agents burst
in on Mark Trail's poaching operation.

Fortunately for Sparky, Zeke knew the famous
"Rex maneuver."

"He kids me … he kids me not. … He kids me …
he kids me not. …"

"Hey! You're not lookin' to buy anything, are you?
I think you best just keep movin', buddy."

"Whoa! Mr. Lewis! We don't know what that thing is
or where it came from, but after what happened to
the dog last week, we advise people not to touch it."

"Well, there he goes again. … I suppose I shouldn't
worry, but I just get a bad feeling about
Jimmy hanging with those tuna punks."

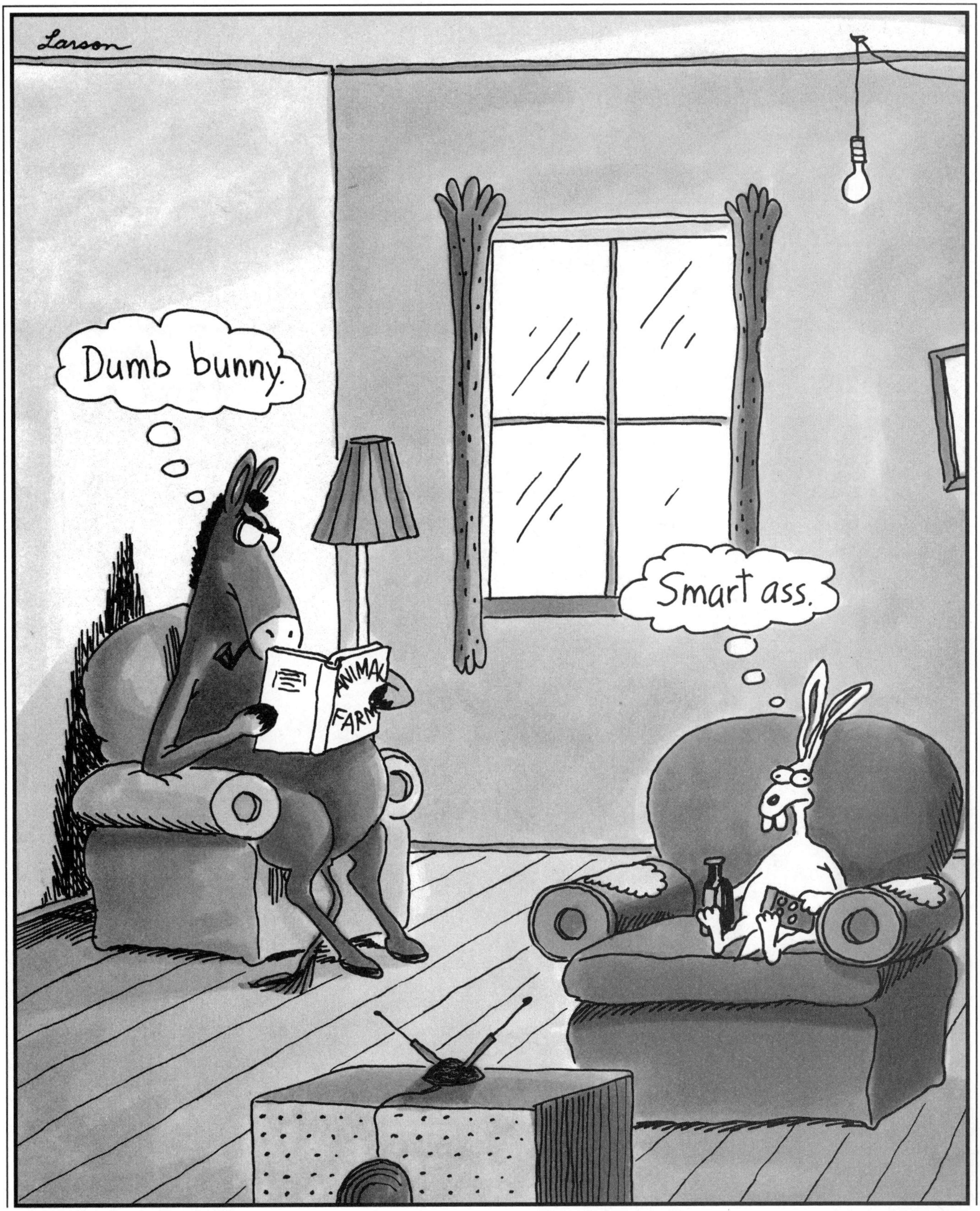
Larson
Dumb bunny.
ANIMAL FARM
Smart ass.

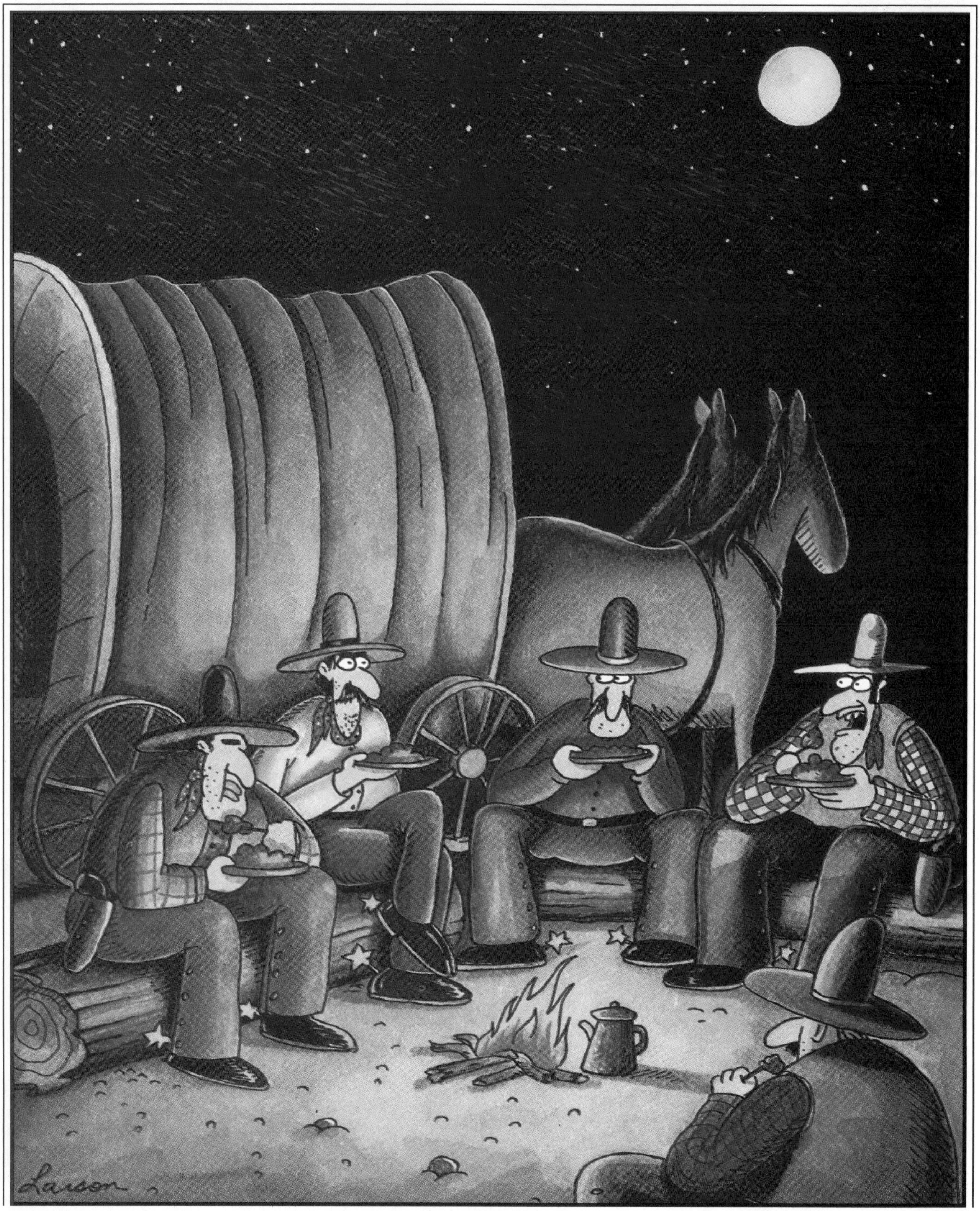
Larson

"Frank … don't do that."

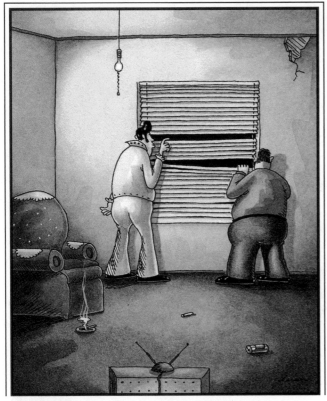

Roommates Elvis and Salman Rushdie sneak a quick look at the outside world.

Carl "Javahead" Jones and his chopped espresso maker

Vera looked around the room. Not another chicken anywhere. And then it struck her—this was a hay bar.

"Well, we're ready for the males' 100-meter freestyle, and I think we can rest assured that most of these athletes will select the dog paddle."

Custer's recurrent nightmare

That night, Captain MacIntyre was killed by a
following sea.

"Now now now. ... You won't be a
lonely road forever, you know."

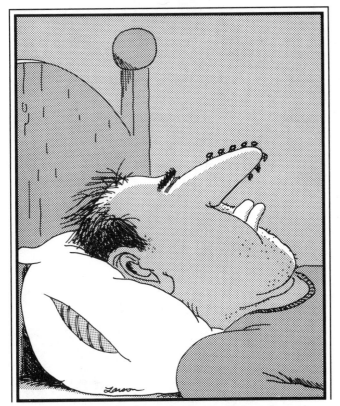

Every August, the fleas would test their endurance
in the grueling Tour de Frank.

WOOOOOOSHHHHHH

To the horror of the lifeboat's other members,
Madonna loses her balance and falls on her face.

"I'm afraid we're going to have to head back, folks. ...
We've got a warning light on up here, and darn
if it isn't the big one."

The woods were dark and foreboding, and Alice sensed
that sinister eyes were watching her every step. Worst
of all, she knew that Nature abhorred a vacuum.

"Confession time, Mona: I've led you astray."

Tensions mount on the Lewis and Clark expedition.

"Amazing! The mummified remains of a prehistoric
cave-painter—still clutching his brush! ...
Seems he made an enemy, though."

Near misses of the Old West

Early plumbers

Calf delinquents

"OK, ma'am, you said you warned your husband to put the newspaper down or you'd blow him away. ... Did he respond?"

"Hey, boy! How ya doin'? ... Look at him, Dan. Poor guy's been floating out here for days but he's still just as fat and happy as ever."

At Slow Cheetahs Anonymous

Red Cloud's ultimate nightmare

Years later, Harold Zimmerman, the original "Hookhand" of campfire ghost stories, tells his grandchildren the Tale of the Two Evil Teen-agers.

As his eyes grew accustomed to the dark, Death suddenly noticed his girlfriend sitting with Dr. Jack Kevorkian.

"Well, lemme think. ... You've stumped me, son. Most folks only wanna know how to go the other way."

"Oh, my God! Dung beetles! ... And in their filthy dungarees, of course!"

"It's a buzzard picnic, son—and you best remember to nary take a look inside one of them baskets."

"... And so the bartender says, 'Hey! That's not a soup spoon!' ... But seriously, forks ..."

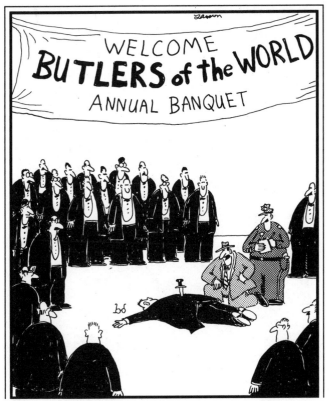

"God, Collings, I hate to start a Monday
with a case like this."

And for the rest of his life, Ernie told his friends
that he had talked with God.

"Hey! You! … Yeah, you! I ain't gonna tell you again!
Quit spittin' on me!"

"Oh, man! The coffee's *cold*!
They thought of *everything*!"

In the corridors of Clowngress

It was no place for yellow squash.

It had been a wonderfully successful day, and the dugout was filled with the sound of laughter and the fruits of their hunting skills. Only Kimbu wore a scowl, returning home with just a single knucklehead.

She was known as Madame D'Gizarde, and, in the early '40s, she used deceit, drugs, and her beguiling charms to become the bane of chicken farmers everywhere.

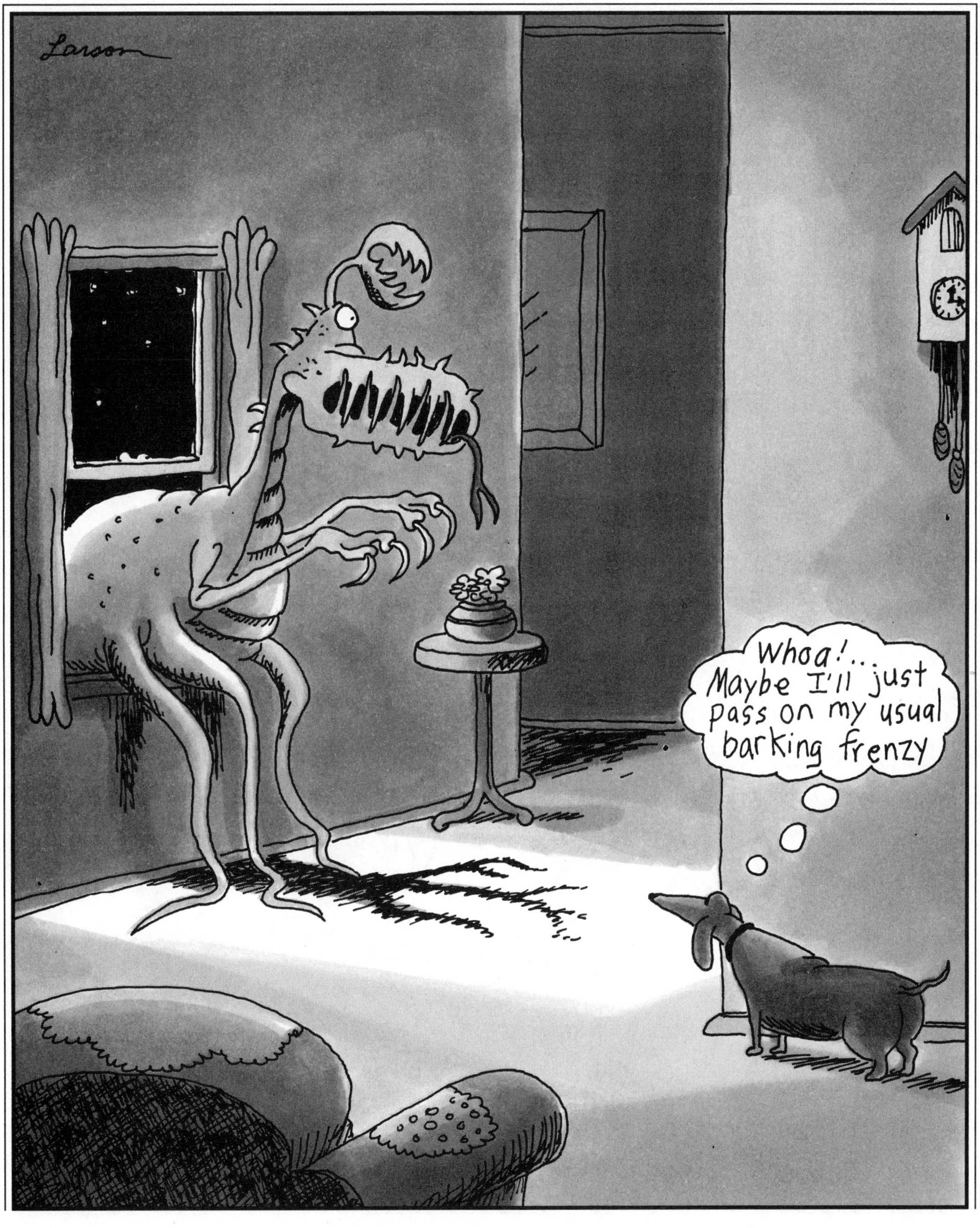
Larson
Whoa!.. Maybe I'll just pass on my usual barking frenzy

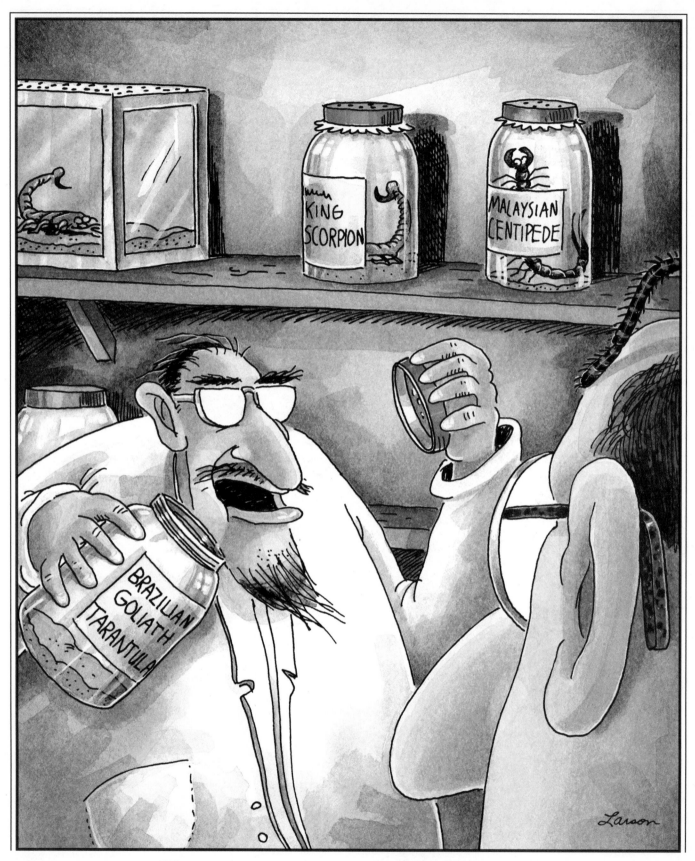

"There you are, my darling ... Rawlings! Don't move!"

Henry VIII on the dating scene

Jurassic calendars

Unbeknownst to most ornithologists, the dodo was actually a very advanced species, living alone quite peacefully until, in the 17th century, it was annihilated by men, rats, and dogs. As usual.

"Most interesting, ma'am—you've identified the defendant as the one you saw running from the scene. I take it, then, that you're unaware that my client is a *walking* stick?"

"Oh, my God, Rogers! ... Is that? ... Is that? ... It is!
It's the *mummy's purse!*"

"The problem, as I see it, is that you both are extremely adept at pushing each other's buttons."

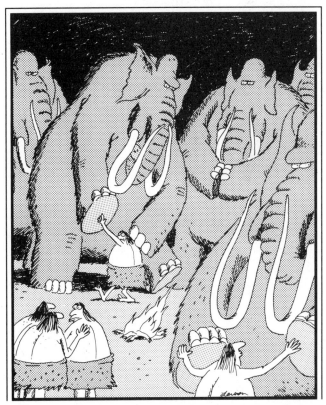

Tomorrow, they would be mortal enemies. But on the eve of the great hunt, feelings were put aside for the traditional Mammoth Dance.

"Face it, Fred—you're lost!"

The Angel of Migraines

Only Claire, with her oversized brain,
wore an expression of concern.

Suddenly the Mensa partygoers froze when Clarence
shockingly uttered the "D" word.

On the air with "Snake Talk"

Special commuter lanes

"Well, I'll be. ... I must've been holding the
dang work order like *this*!"

"OK, boys—that'll be enough.
We don't allow any gunplay in this town."

God at His computer

The art of conversation

He had seen Tanzania, and most of Mozambique was
already behind him. There was no mistake. Chippy had
done what most chimps only dream about:
He had caught the Perfect Vine.

"OK, OK! Calm down, everyone! ... This monster—
would you say he was bigger or smaller than your
building? ... You can talk it over."

Punk worms

Hell's video store

"One more time: You were at the park, enjoying the afternoon, when you distinctly heard the defendant turn to his dog and say: 'Look, boy! A stickman!'"

"Boy, everyone's really out wandering the streets tonight. ... I tell you, Charles, we're getting to be real home zombies."

Where the deer and the antelope work

At the monthly meeting of Squidheads Anonymous

"Yeah. I remember Jerry. Good friend of mine. ... You know, I never understood a single word he said, but he always had some mighty fine wine."

In what was destined to be a short-lived spectacle, a chicken, suspended by a balloon, floated through the Samurai bar's doorway.

"Hey! ... You!"

The curse of songwriter's block

"Thanks for being my friend, Wayne."

"Oh, the box of dead flies? Ramone gave them to me
Saturday night during his courtship display. ...
Of course, they were already sucked dry."

Practical jokes of the Paleolithic

"My marriage is in trouble, Barbara. You ever tried communicating with a hammerhead?"

"You *must* be new here! ... That's Miss Crutchfield, and she's there to make sure *nobody* runs with scissors."

"Of course, one of the most popular myths is that our 16th president was born in a little log cabin."

" … And please let Mom, Dad, Rex, Ginger, Tucker,
me, and all the rest of the family see color."

"Look here, McGinnis—hundreds of bright copper kettles, warm woolen mittens, brown paper packages tied up with string. ... Someone was after a few of this guy's favorite things."

Scene from *Dr. Jekyll and Mr. Ed*

Failed marketing ploys

"Go ahead and jump, Sid! Hell—I *know* you're thinkin' it!"

"Look. If you're so self-conscious about it, get yourself a gorilla mask."

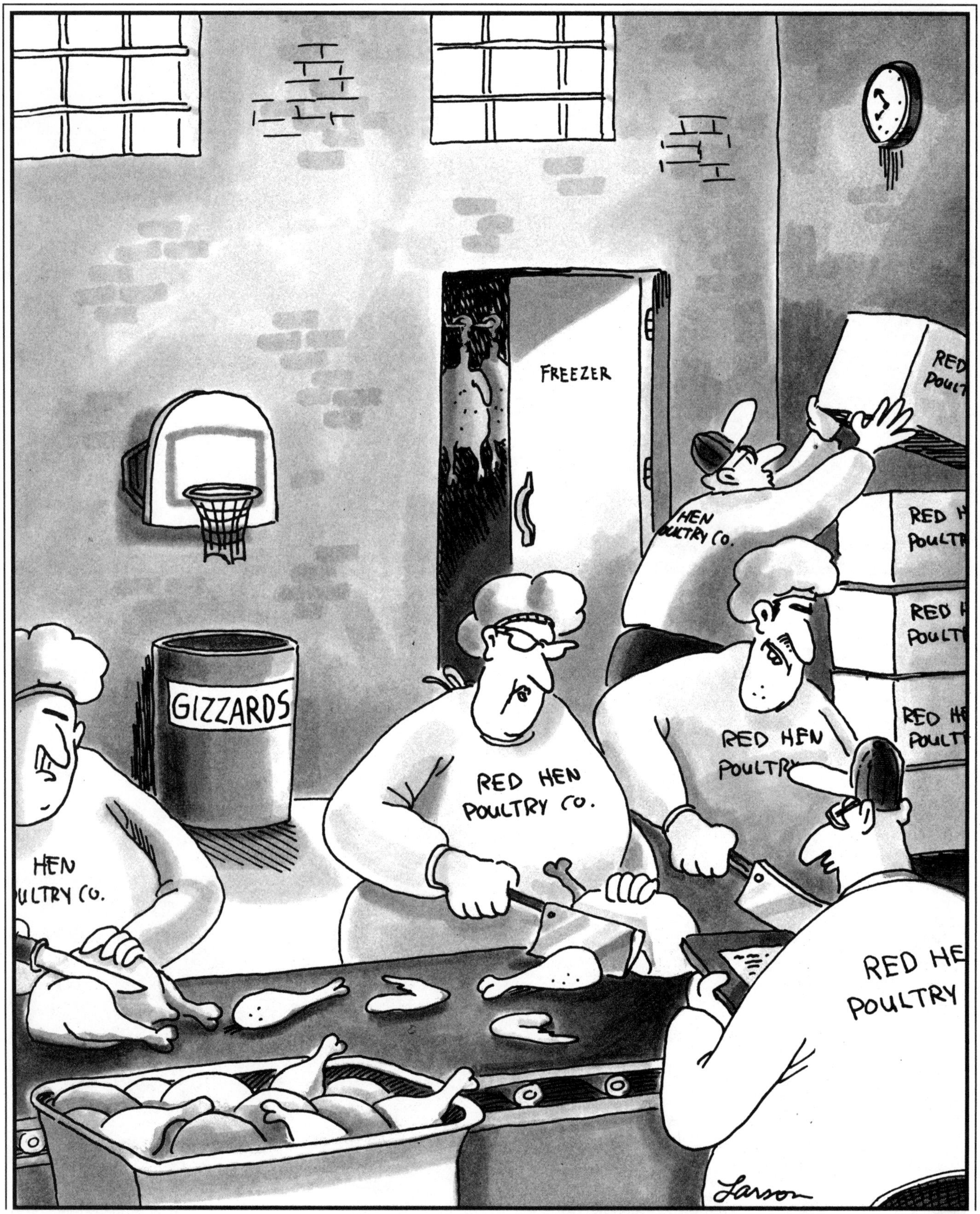
FREEZER
RED POULT
HEN POULTRY CO.
RED H POULTR
RED H POULT
GIZZARDS
RED HEN POULTRY CO.
RED HEN POULTR
RED HE POULT
HEN POULTRY CO.
RED HE POULTRY
Larson

Scene from *Insurance Salesman of the Opera*

Monday night in the woods

"OK, crybaby! You want the last soda?
Well, let me *get it ready* for you!"

"We're screwed, Marge. Big Al was our star attraction,
the king of the show. ... And now he's gone."

"Don't touch it, honey ... it's just a face in the crowd."

Be a virus, see the world.

A tragedy occurs off the coast
of a land called Honah-Lee.

"Quit school? *Quit school?* You wanna end up
like your father? A career lab rat?"

"Look, if it was electric, could I do this?"

Where we get calamari blanc

Three more careers are claimed by the
Bermuda Triangle of jazz.

"Excuse me, sir, but could your entire family please
step out of the car? ... Your faces are not in order."

On this particular day, Rory the raccoon was hunting frogs at his favorite stream, and the pleasant background music told him that Mr. Mountain Lion was nowhere around.

Professor Glickman, the lab practical joker, deftly placed a single drop of hydrochloric acid on the back of Professor Bingham's neck.

"Voila! ... Your new dream home! If you like it, I can get a crew mixing wood fibers and saliva as early as tomorrow."

"Well, kid, ya beat me—and now every punk packin' a paddle and tryin' to make a name for himself will come lookin' for *you*! ... Welcome to hell, kid."

Dog ventriloquists

Boxer nightmares

"Norm? This is Mitch. ...
You were right—I found my drill."

Back in his college days, Igor was considered
to be the HBOC.

54

At the I've Fallen and I Can't Get Up Building

"Tell me, Margaret. ... Am I a butthead?"

"Hey! I got news for you, sweetheart! ...
I *am* the lowest form of life on earth!"

What the stranger didn't know, of course,
was that Sam always kept a dobie in his boot.

For many weeks, the two species had lived in mutual tolerance of one another. And then, without provocation, the hornets began throwing rocks at Ned's house.

"As you can see, most of these things are jackrabbits, but keep your eyes peeled for armadillo as well. ... We're about five miles now from the dead steer."

"It's time we face reality, my friends. ...
We're not exactly rocket scientists."

"That's why I never walk in front."

The magnificent Lippizaner cows

Slave-ship entertainers

"OK, everyone, we'll be departing for Antarctica
in about 15 minutes. ... If anyone thinks he may be
in the wrong migration, let us know now."

As witnesses later recalled, two small dogs just
waltzed into the place, grabbed the cat,
and waltzed out.

Suddenly, the cops stepped into the clearing,
and the Spamshiners knew they were busted.

By blending in with the ostrich's eggs, Hare Krishnas are subsequently raised by the adult birds.

"I lift, you grab. ... Was that concept just a little too complex, Carl?"

Bored dogs are often subject to the phenomenon of cat mirages.

Well, sir, at the time, me and my brother were trying to solve the secret of Pirate's Cove. We had no idea where the whole thing would lead.

Testifying before a Senate subcommittee, the Hardy boys crack the Iran-contra scandal.

Pickpockets of the Rue Morgue

Vern, Chuck, and the pope go fishing

"OK, kids, here we go. ... And I believe Danny's right,
Randy—it's his turn to eat the queen."

Before starting their day, squirrels must first
pump themselves up.

"I love the desert."

Octopus obedience school

"Pardon me, boys—is that the Chattanooga
Iron Horse?"

"Be patient, Leona, be patient. ... Zebras won't take
a drink until they know it's absolutely safe."

Dr. Frankenstein vacations in Hawaii

Tales of the Early Bird

Ironically, Barnum's and Bailey's respective kids—Sid and Marty—both ran away one night to join corporate America.

"Talk about adding insult to injury! Not only did we arrive late, but they *deliberately* left his organ-donor card."

Origin of the expression, "Putting on the dog"

Bored towns of the Old West

"And so," the interviewer asked, "do you ever have trouble coming up with ideas?" "Well, sometimes," the cartoonist replied.

"You gotta help me, Mom. ... This assignment is due tomorrow, and Gramps doesn't understand the new tricks."

The first day at fly summer camp

The ever-popular Donner Party snow dome

"Abdul, my old friend! Come in, come in!
Have you traveled far?!"

Hummingbirds, of course, have to watch nature films
with the action greatly speeded up.

Incredibly, Morty had forgotten to bring a pocketbook.

"Time out, please! ... Eyelash!"

"Little Bear! A watched head
never gets eaten by ants."

Question: If a tree falls in the forest and no one's
around, and it hits a mime, does anyone care?

Everything was starting to come into focus for Farmer MacDougal—his missing sheep, his missing beer, and his collie, Shep, who was getting just a little too sociable for his own good.

"You're a right-brained sort of person, Mr. Sommersby—*very* creative, artistic, etc. ... Unfortunately, I think I also see why you're having trouble figuring out your gas mileage."

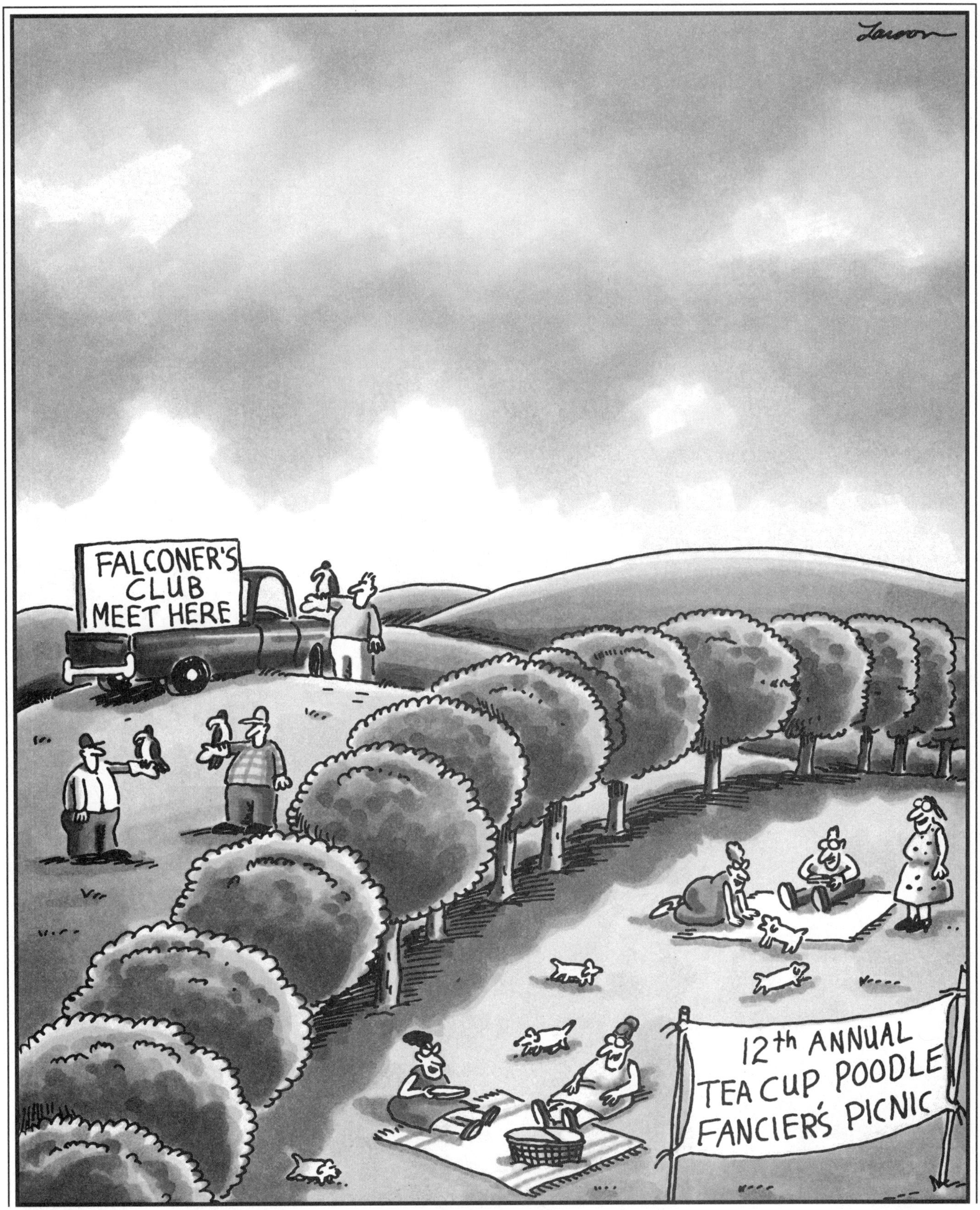
FALCONER'S CLUB MEET HERE
12th ANNUAL TEA CUP POODLE FANCIER'S PICNIC

Trouble brewing

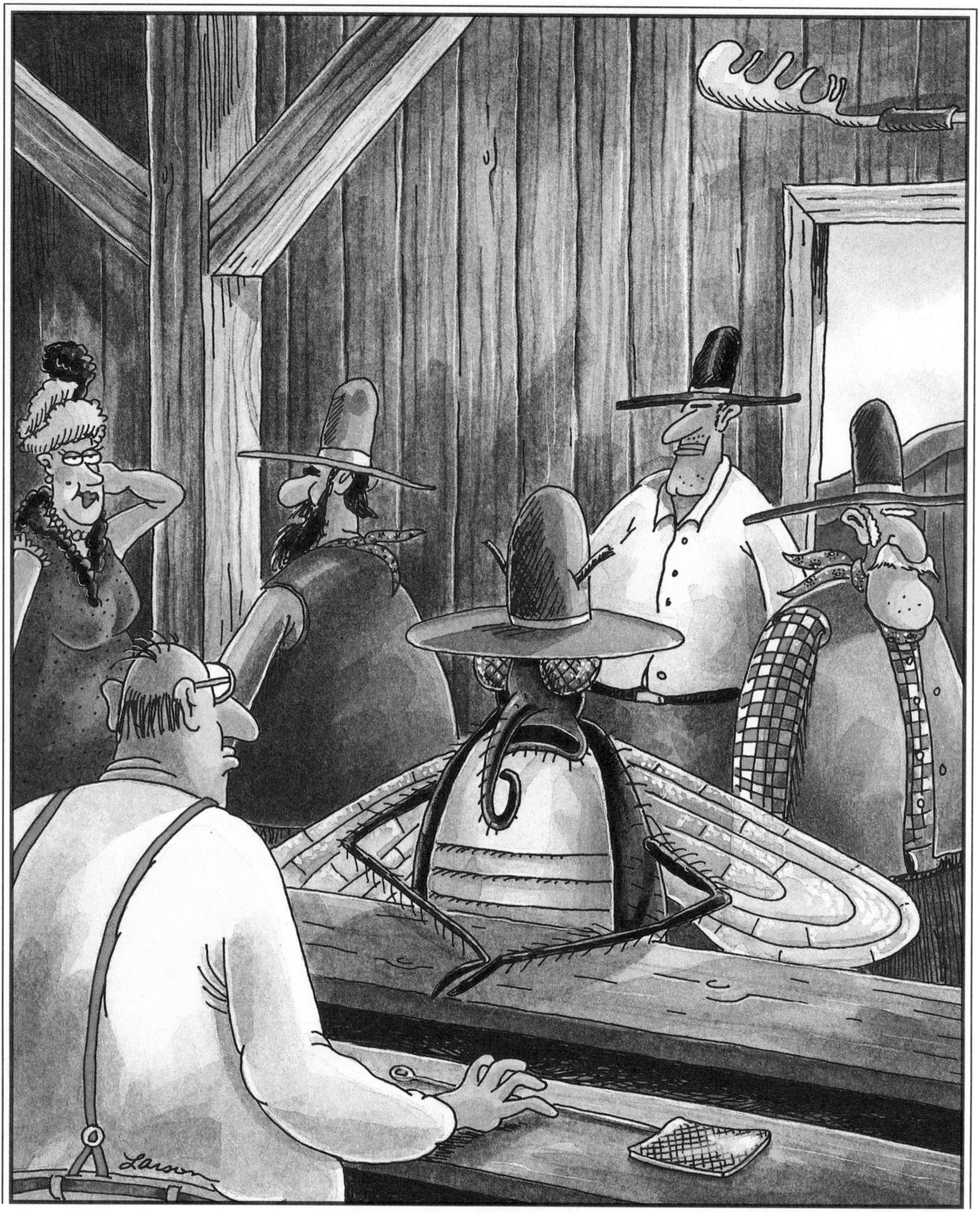
Larson

"I wouldn't do that, bartender. … Unless, of course, you think you're fast enough."

The Ice Crusades

"Oo! *I'd* get up on that big fuzzy one!"

"Professor LaVonne had many enemies in the entomological world, detective, but if you examine that data label, you'll find exactly when and where he was—shall we say—'collected.'"

Historical note: For many years, until they became truly nasty, Vikings would plunder, loot, and then egg the houses of coastal villagers.

At the Insurance Agents Wax Museum

A big day for Jimmy

"Hey, you'll love it! All she needs is some gravel, a few plants, and maybe one of those miniature human skeletons."

Early corsages

The living hell of Maurice, Jacques Cousteau's cat

Crucial decisions along life's highway

Stumpy didn't know how he got in this situation, but with the whole town watching, he knew he'd have to play it out.

"OK, time for lunch. ... And Dwayne here will be dismissing you by row number, since he's alpha wolf today."

Abducted by an alien circus company, Professor Doyle is forced to write calculus equations in center ring.

"Oh, it's just Hank's little cross to bear—he's allergic to down and that's that."

In her past, and unbeknownst to most people, Leona Helmsley was an avid bungee jumper.

Ichabod Crane vs. the Headless Horseman in The People's Court

And then the bovine watchers were given a *real* treat. On a small knoll, in full splendor, there suddenly appeared a Guatemalan cow of paradise.

"Oh, yeah! Well, I'd rather be a living corpse made from dismembered body parts than a hunchbacked little grave robber like you!"

Prairie dog developers

More trouble brewing

Long before his show-business career, he was known
as *Mr.* Liberace, the wood-shop teacher.

"Listen, Noreen—*you* wanna be the
photographer next time, be my guest."

"Oh, yeah? Well, maybe I'll just come over there and rattle *your* cage!"

With the surgical team passed out, and with help from the observation deck, hospital custodian Leonard Knudson suddenly became responsible for bringing Mr. Gruenfeld "home."

More facts of nature: All forest animals, to this very day, remember exactly where they were and what they were doing when they heard that Bambi's mother had been shot.

"So, Mr. Pig—you built that fire *after* you heard my client coming down your chimney! ... Did you know my client is an endangered species, Mr. Pig, while you yourself are nothing more than a walking side of ham?"

Long before his rise to fame, artist Gus Nickerson experimented with many variations on a single theme— until that fateful day when a friend said, "Gus ... have you tried *dogs* playing poker?"

"Well, yes, that is the downside, Fluffy. ... When we kill her, the pampering will end."

"The dentist just buzzed me, Mrs. Lewellyn—he's ready to see Bobby now."

Winning the lottery had changed his life, but at times Chico still felt strangely unfulfilled.

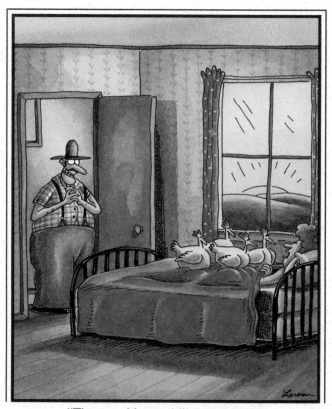

"This is it, Maurice! I've warned you to keep your hens off me!"

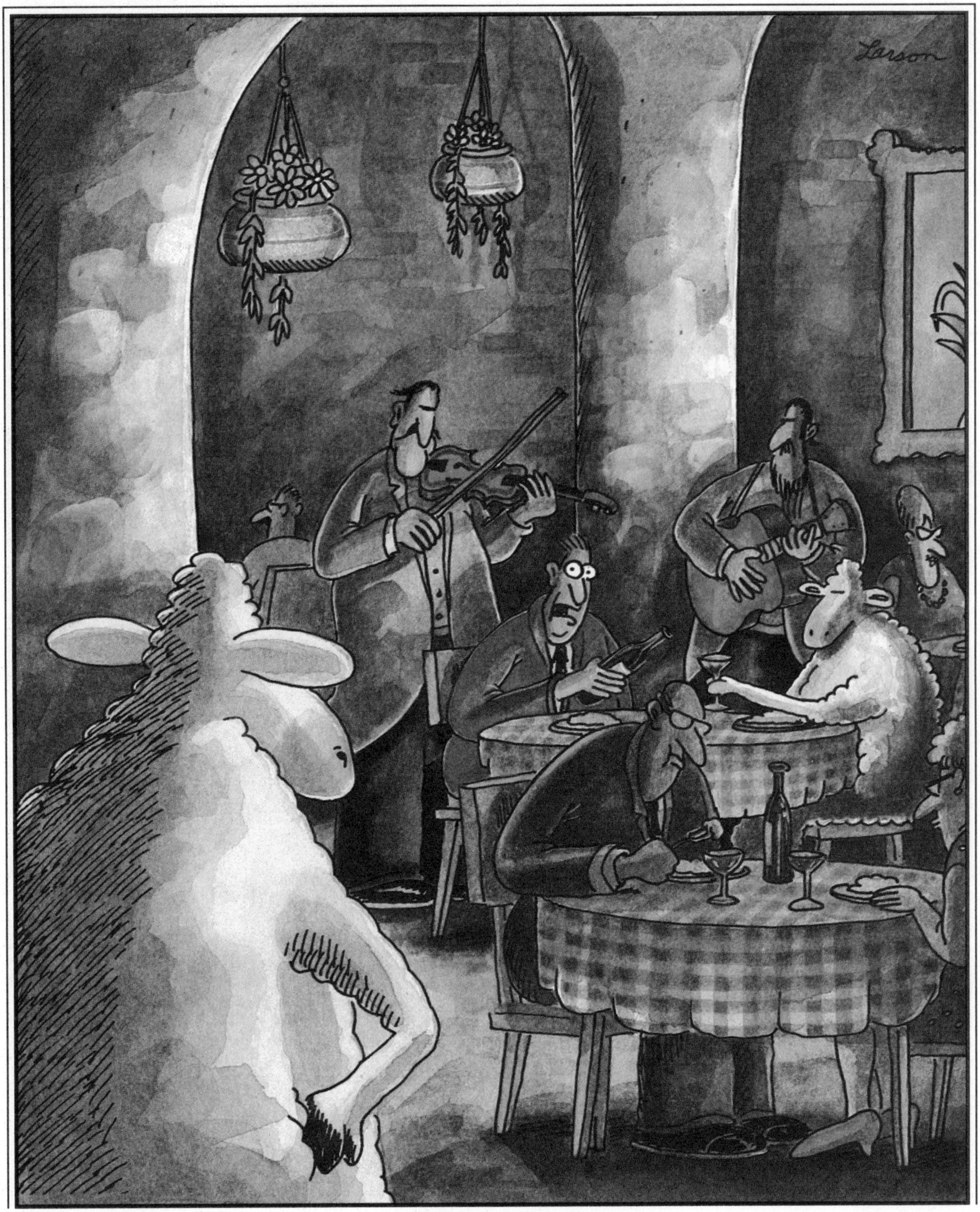
Larson

"Oh my God! It's Yvonne!"

"*His* story? Well, I dunno. ... I always assumed he was just a bad dog."

Vegetarian towns of the Old West

The Viking longcar was once the scourge of
European roadways.

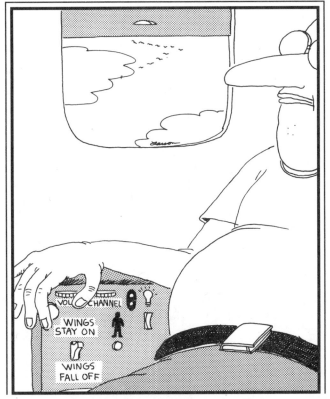

Fumbling for his recline button, Ted
unwittingly instigates a disaster.

While vacationing in Africa, Pinocchio has his
longtime wish to be a real boy suddenly and
unexpectedly granted.

Acts of God

Giorgio Armani at home

"I tell ya, Ben—no matter who wins this thing,
Boot Hill ain't ever gonna be the same."

Where the respective worlds of boating
and herpetology converge.

Zoombies: the driving dead

"I dunno, Andy. ... Mom said we were never to go near the old Sutter place."

Misunderstanding his dying father's advice, Arnie spent several years protecting the family mules.

"Edgar! Leave him be! ... Always best to let sleeping dogs lie."

Popeye on the dating scene

"Latte, Jed?"

Of course, prehistoric neighborhoods always had
that one family whose front yard was strewn with old
mammoth remains.

Unbeknownst to most students of psychology,
Pavlov's first experiment was to ring a bell and
cause his dog to attack Freud's cat.

"AAAAAAAAA! It's Sid! Someone snuffed him!"

How poodles first came to North America

"Well, I'd recommend either the chicken-fried steak or maybe the seafood platter. But look—I gotta be honest with ya—nothin' we serve is exactly what I'd call food for the gods."

Expatriates, they migrated in the 1920s to Paris' Left Bank, gathering in their favorite haunts and discussing the meaning of cream pies and big shoes. They were, in fact, the original Boclownians.

It was a tough frontier town; but later, after the arrival of the Earp brothers, things calmed down, and the town's name was shortened to simply Dodge City.

Chicken sexual fantasies

"Now watch your step, Osborne. ... The Squiggly Line people have an inherent distrust for all smoothliners."

Again the doorbell chimed. With his wife out of town, and not expecting any visitors, Mohammed began to grow uneasy.

It was an innocent mistake, but nevertheless, a moment later Maurice found himself receiving the full brunt of the mummy's wrath.

Cornered and sensing danger, Sidney flares his "eye spots."

"I hate 'em. They mess on the stools, they attack the mirror—and, of course, they drink like birds."

"Yeah, Vern! You heard what I said! And what are you gonna do about it? Huh? C'mon! What are ya gonna do? Huh? *C'mon!*"

The class abruptly stopped practicing. Here was an opportunity to not only employ their skills, but also to save the entire town.

Darren was unaware that, under the table, his wife and Raymond were playing "tentaclies."

And then Al realized his problems were much bigger than just a smashed truck.

"Whoa! Whoa! C'mon, you guys! This is just a friendly game of cards—ease up on those acid-filled beakers."

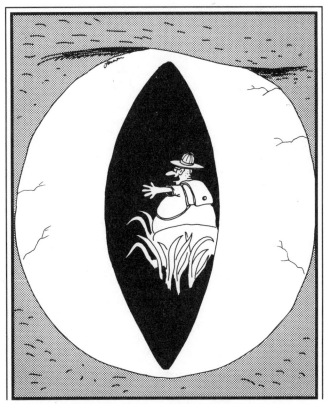

"My gun, Desmond! I sense this striped man-eater is somewhere dead ahead, waiting to ambush us! ... Ohhhhhh, he thinks he's so clever."

Tarantula coffeehouses

"Oooooo! Check it out, Edith! It's a *quadra*ceratops!"

Every year, hundreds of tourists travel great distances to get a glimpse of the few remaining mountain chihuahuas.

"You were hit last night by some cult, Mr. Gilbert. ... Not the sickest cult I've ever seen, but a cult nonetheless."

Charlie Brown in Indian country

Some of our more common "rescue" animals

Although never achieving the fame of his African counterpart, Larry of the Lemurs was a common sight to natives of Madagascar.

"OK, Mr. Hook. Seems you're trying to decide between a career in pirating or massage therapy. Well, maybe we can help you narrow it down."

Unwittingly, Raymond wanders into the hive's company picnic.

"And then wham! This thing just came right out of left field."

Wellington held out some beads and other trinkets, but the islanders had sent their fiercest lawyers—some of whom were chanting, "Sue him! Sue him!

The herd moved in around him, but Zach had known better than to approach these animals without his trusty buffalo gum.

Tension mounts in the final heat of the
paper-rock-scissors event.

Once again, Vernon has a good shirt ruined by
a cheap pocket octopus.

"A word of advice, Durk: It's the Mesolithic. We've
domesticated the dog, we're using stone tools,
and no one's *naked* anymore."

"New guy, huh? Well, up here, you walk the *edge*!
And the edge is a fickle hellcat. ... Love her, but
never trust her, for her heart is full of *lye*!"

Classic conversation stoppers

Primitive theme parks

That night, their revenge was meted out on both
Farmer O'Malley and his wife. The next day, police
investigators found a scene that they could describe
only as "grisly, yet strangely hilarious."

A few days following the King Kong "incident,"
New Yorkers return to business as usual.

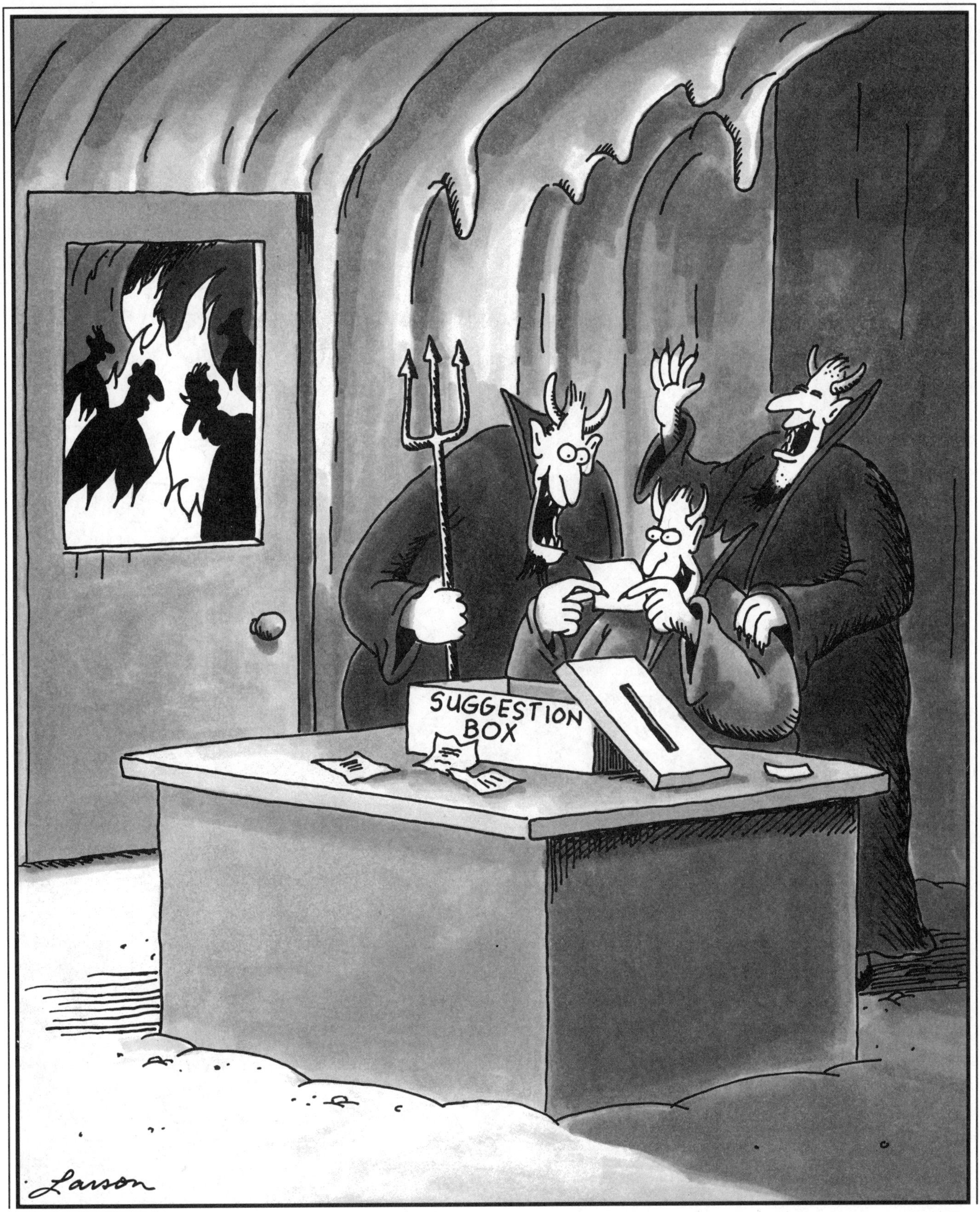
SUGGESTION BOX
Larson

"OK, Professor Big Mouth, we've all chipped in. Here's the hundred bucks, but remember—you gotta kiss her on the *lips*!"

In an effort to show off, the monster would sometimes stand on his head.

"Well, there goes Binky with the boss again. ... What a red-noser!"

It was always a bizarre spectacle, but no one ever, ever, ridiculed the Teapot Kid.

Daffy's résumé

Entomological rodeos

Later, when one of the monsters cranked up the
volume, the party really got going.

"It's Jim Wilkins, Dave. Same as the others. Trussed
up like a Christmas present with his hunting license
stuffed in his mouth. ... I want this bear, Dave.
I want him bad."

Eskimo rescue units

"Well, I've got good gnus and I've got bad gnus."

"Oh, God! It's that creepy Ted Sheldon and Louise Dickerson. ... They're skinkheads, you know."

After being frozen in ice for 10,000 years, Thag promotes his autobiography.

Scotty in hell

At the Vatican's movie theater

"Could you come back later?
He's catching a few Y's right now."

Fortunately, even the Boy Scouts who
fail knot-tying get to go camping.

"Smash your left hand down about right here three times, then twice up in this area, then three times right about here. ... That's 'Louie Louie.'"

Zeke froze. For the longest time, all he could do was stare at the chocolate mint that "someone" had placed on his bedroll.

Summoned by the gonging, Professor Crutchfeld stepped into the clearing. The little caterpillars had done well this time in their offering.

The entire parliament fell dead silent. For the first time since anyone could remember, one of the members voted "aye."

Raymond's last day as the band's sound technician

Jurassic parking

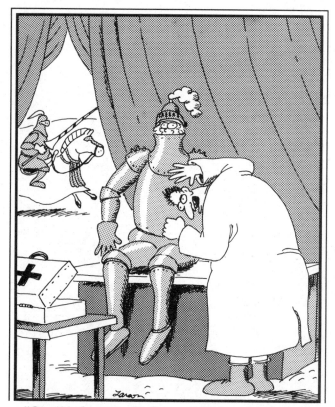

"Ooo! You're right, Sir Dwayne! If I knock right here,
I can make him start buzzing. ... Ooo, and he's *angry*!"

"This is it, son—my old chompin' grounds. ...
Gosh, the memories."

"Just keep starin', buddy, and
I'll show ya my *bad* eye!"

Iggy knew he was extremely lucky
to get a room with a view.

"Good heavens! Pablo got an 'F' in art! ... Well, I'm
just going to go down to that school myself and meet
this teacher face to face!"

"OK, I got one—do you say 'darn it' or 'dern it'?"

Backing out of the driveway, Mr. Peabody suddenly brought his car to a stop. He had already heard a peculiar "thump," and now these flattened but familiar-looking glasses further intrigued him.

"And then one of the little kids shined his flashlight into the corner of the basement, and there they saw these strange jars. ... Some said 'creamy,' some said 'crunchy' ..."

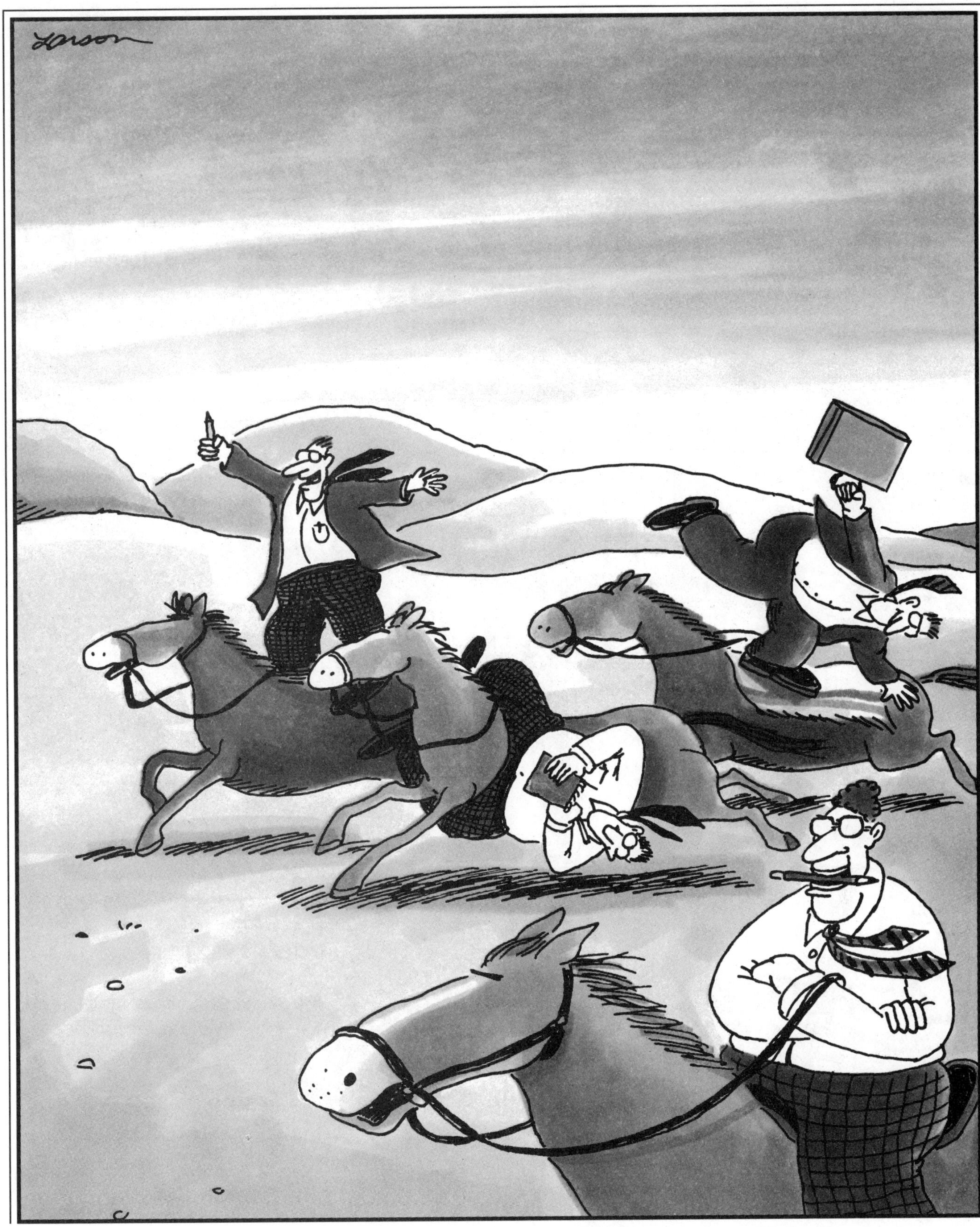
Larson

Cossaccountants

Later, Edna was forced to sell her brussels sprout house.

Moses parting his hair

Clark's mother

"Come with us, ma'am—and if I were you, I'd get a good lawyer. No one's gonna buy that my-husband-was-only-hibernating story."

"Remember, Calloway, this is their biggest and best warrior—so stay alert! When you knock him down, he's going to come right back at you!"

Some wolves, their habitat destroyed and overwhelmed by human pressures, turn to snorting quack.

"No, no. … Not this one. Too many bells and whistles."

"I've been told you don't like my dirt!"

"Dang it, Morty! … You're always showing this picture of me you took at 7 o'clock in the morning!"

"Hey! *You* don't tell *me* what makes 'er tick! *I* know what makes 'er tick, sonny boy!"

Midget westerns

Specialized obituaries

"I'm sorry, sir, but the reservation book simply says 'Jason.' ... There's nothing here about Jason *and* the Argonauts."

Professor Ferrington and his controversial theory that dinosaurs were actually the discarded "chicken" bones of giant, alien picnickers.

"That's him. Second from the end—the 12-footer!"

"Today, our guest lecturer is Dr. Clarence Tibbs, whose 20-year career has culminated in his recent autobiography, *Zoo Vet—I Quit!*"

"Vera! Come quick! Some nature show has a hidden camera in the Ericksons' burrow! ... We're going to see their entire courtship behavior!"

"It's OK! Dart not poisonous. ...
Just showin' my kid the ropes!"

After many years of marital bliss,
tension enters the Kent household.

"I *would* have gotten away scot free if I had just gotten
rid of the evidence. ... But, shoot—I'm a packrat."

For the time being, the monster wasn't
in Ricky's closet. For the time being.

In medieval times, a suit of armor often
served as a family's message center.

It's a known fact that the sheep that give
us steel wool have no natural enemies.

The Sandwich Mafia sends Luigi to
"sleep with the fourth-graders."

"Oh, Professor DeWitt! Have you seen Professor
Weinberg's time machine? ... It's digital!"

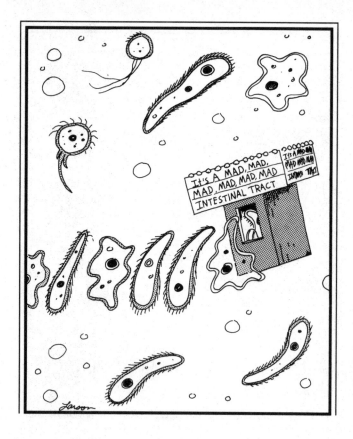

"My God, Carlson! After years of searching, this is an emotional moment for me! ... Voilà! I give you the Secret Elephant Breeding Grounds!"

In the stadiums of ancient Rome, the most feared trial was the rub-your-stomach-and-pat-your-head-at-the-same-time event.

Monster game shows

The Wildlife Management finals

"Sorry, son, but for you to understand what happened, you have to first understand that back in the '60s we were all taking a lot of drugs."

"Now if you all would examine the chart, you will notice—well, well … seems Mr. Sparky has found something more engrossing than this meeting."

Basic field trips

Primitive mail fraud

"Oh, and a word of warning about Mueller over there. ... He's got a good head on his shoulders, but it's best not to mention it."

"It's a cute trick, Warren, but the Schuberts are here for dinner, so just 'abracadabra' this thing back to where it was."

"Mmmmmm ... interesting ... interesting. ... I'd say we taste a little like chicken."

"Struck from behind, all right ... and from my first examination of the wound,
I'd say this was done by some kind of heavy, blunt object."

"Hey, Lola. Did you see this thing in the paper?"

Scorpion school

Careening through the neighborhood with
reckless abandon, none of them suspected that
Tuffy was still tied up.

"Sheriff! Ben Wiggins is ridin' into town,
and he's wearin' that same little chiffon number
that he wore when he shot Jake Sutton!"

"Whoa! ... Think I found the problem, buddy."

"The truth is, Stan, I'd like a place of my own."

...and as I go, I love to sing, my knapsack on my back! Valderi, valdera, valderi, valdera ha ha ha ha ha ...

God, I hate him.

More tension on the Lewis and Clark expedition.

Arrrrrrrgh! Arrrrgh! Arrrrrrrrrgh!

Zuppo?...Zuppah?... Dang! This one's hard!... Zippo?...Zippuh?... Zipper! Yes, that's it! Zipper!

Professor Wainwright's painstaking field research to decode the language of bears comes to a sudden and horrific end.

"Whoa! Another bad one! ... I see your severed head lying quietly in the red-stained dirt, a surprised expression still frozen in your lifeless eyes. ... Next."

"We don't know exactly who he is, Captain—
a disgruntled worker, we figure."

"Hey, we'll be lucky if we *ever* sell this place! ... Well,
it's like everyone says—location, location, location."

"Eat my apple, will you? *Leave my garden!*
Begone! ... And take all the mole traps with you!"

Christmas morning 1837: Santa Anna's son, Juan,
receives the original Davy Crockett hat.

The party was going along splendidly—and then Morty opened the door to the wolverine display.

"I'm sorry, Sidney, but I can no longer help you. ... These are not my people."

"It's the only way to go, Frank. Why, my life's changed, ever since I discovered Stackable Livestock.®"

"And now the weather—well, doggone it, but I'm afraid that cold front I told you about yesterday is just baaarrreeely going to miss us."

Sheep that pass in the night

"Let's see...You make fire--good... You make tools--good...You hunt mammoth...okaaaaaay...Uh-oh! Your references are all baboons--not good."

Primitive résumés

"Well, actually, Doreen, I rather resent being called a 'swamp thing.' ... I prefer the term 'wetlands-challenged mutant.'"

"Hey! So I made the wrong decision! ... But you know, I really wasn't sure I *wanted* to swing on a star, carry moonbeams home in a jar!"

Centaur rodeos

Theater of the Gods

"Oh, Misty always hates me showing this slide. ...
It's halftime at the '88 Detroit-Chicago
game when we met."

Douglas is ejected from the spoon band.

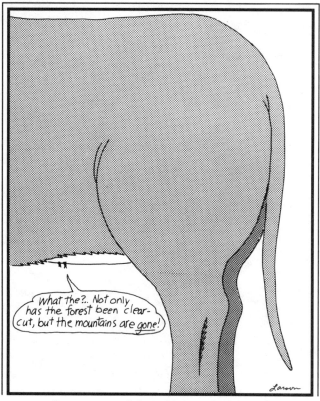

Environmental disasters in a flea's world

"So George says, 'I'm goin' over there and tellin' that guy to shut that equipment off!' ... So I said: 'George, that guy's a mad scientist. Call the cops. Don't go over there alone.' ... Well, you know what George did."

Thirty years had passed, and although he had no real regrets about marrying Wendy, buying a home, and having two kids, Peter found his thoughts often going back to his life in Never-Never-Land.

Mike Wallace interviews the Devil.

"So let's go over it again: You're about a mile up, you see something dying below you, you circle until it's dead, and down you go. Lenny, you stick close to your brothers and do what they do."

"Well, this guidebook is worthless! It just says these people worshipped two gods: one who was all-knowing and one who was all-seeing—but they don't tell you which is which, for crying out loud!"

In Saddam Hussein's war room

God designs the great white shark

"Well, as usual, there goes Princess Luwana—always
the center of attention. ... You know, underneath that
outer wrap, she's held together with duct tape."

He was king of the sheep.

Back home in his native India, Toomba tells and retells the story
of his daring escape from the Cleveland Zoo.

"And down here we keep Fluffy. ... We're afraid he may have gone mad."

Carl had never had so much fun in his whole life, and he knew, from this moment on, that he would never again be a lone pine tree.

"Margaret! You? ... I ... I ... should ... have ... knowwwwwnnnnn ..."

"Sorry, ma'am, but your neighbors have reported not seeing your husband in weeks. We just have a few questions, and then you can get back to your canning."

Inside tours of Acme Fake Vomit Inc.

"Bad guy comin' in, Arnie! ... Minor key!"

"Listen up, my Cossack brethren! We'll ride into the valley like the wind, the thunder of our horses and the lightning of our steel striking fear in the hearts of our enemies! ... And remember—stay out of Mrs. Caldwell's garden!"

"So, Professor Sadowsky, you're saying that your fellow researcher, Professor Lazzell, knowing full well that baboons consider eye contact to be threatening, handed you this hat on that fateful day you emerged from your Serengeti campsite."

Sumo temporaries

Humboys

For a long time, Farmer Hansen and his tall chickens
enjoyed immense popularity—until Farmer Sutton
got himself a longcow.

High above the hushed crowd, Rex tried to remain
focused. Still, he couldn't shake one nagging thought:
He was an old dog and this was a new trick.

History shmistory

Clown therapy sessions

"Well, I'll be darned. Says here 70 percent of all accidents happen in the hole."

"Well, time for our weekly brain-stem-storming session."

Scene from *Cape Buffalo Fear*

Alert, but far from panicked, the herbivores studied the sudden arrival of two cheetah speedwalkers.

"Oh, my word, Helen! You play, *too*? ... And here I always thought you were just a songbird."

Vacationing from their jobs of terrorizing young teen-agers, zombies will often relax at a Western dead ranch.

Beverly Hills of the North Pole

"Well, first the bad news—you're definitely hooked."

A Louvre guard is suddenly unsettled by
the arrival of Linda Blair.

"We can't go on like this, Ramone. ... One day,
George is bound to take his blinders off."

Medieval chicken coops

Donning his new canine decoder, Professor Schwartzman becomes the first human being on Earth to hear what barking dogs are actually saying.

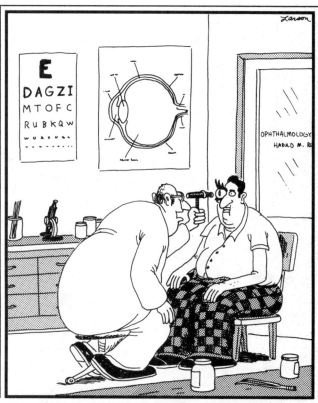

"Oh, this is wonderful, Mr. Gruenfeld—I've only seen it a couple of times. You have corneal corruption. ... Evil eye, Mr. Gruenfeld, evil eye."

Concepts of hell

"Well, I'm not sure if we can afford stomach insurance—right now we're trying to put the kids through the small intestine."

Early checkers

145

Abraham Lincoln's first car

"Lassie! ... come home! ... Lassie come home!"

The questions were getting harder, and Ted could feel Lucky's watchful glare from across the room. He had been warned, he recalled, that this was a breed that would sometimes test him.

"So please welcome our keynote speaker, Professor Melvin Fenwick—the man who, back in 1952, first coined the now common phrase: 'Fools! I'll destroy them all!'"

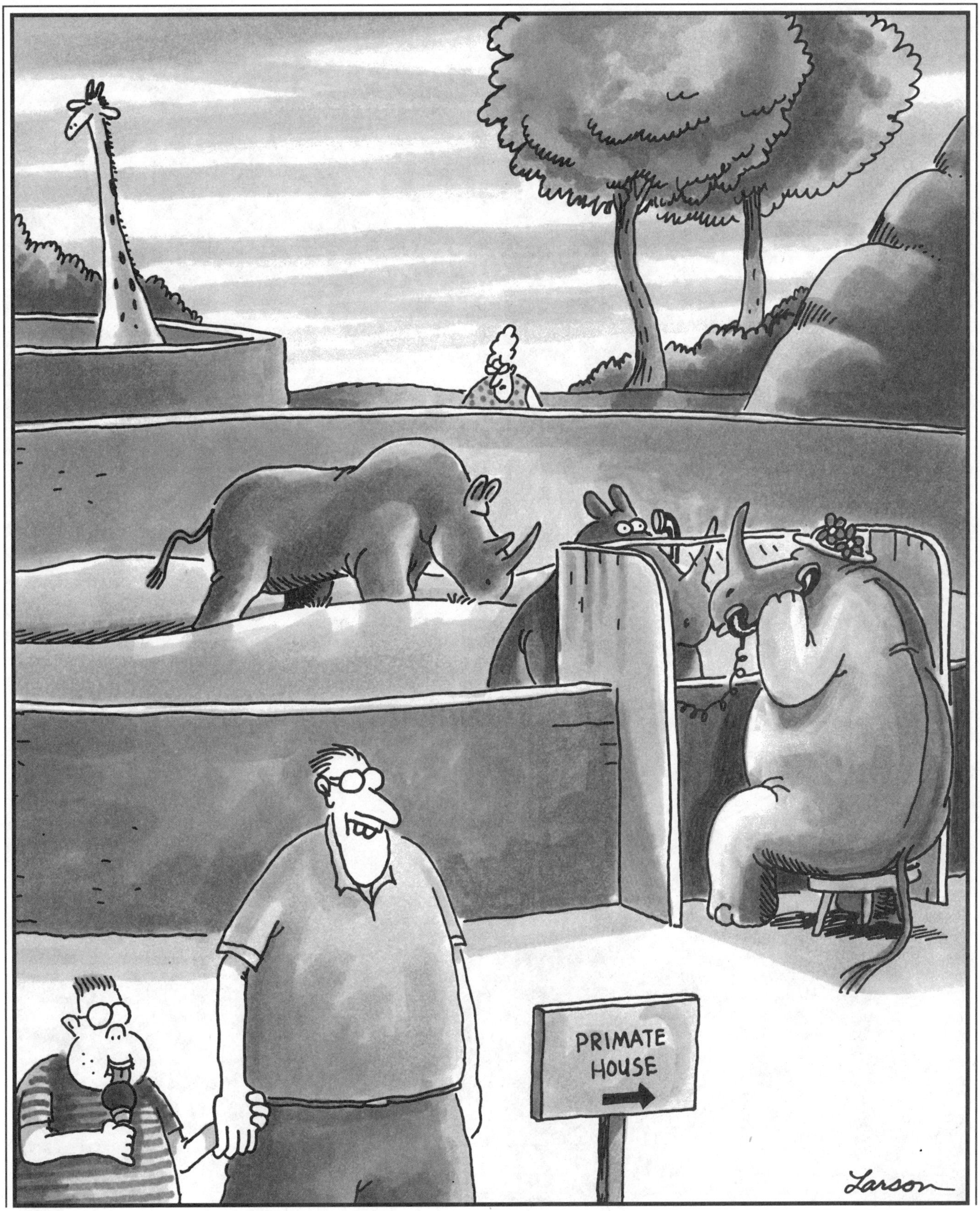
PRIMATE HOUSE
Larson

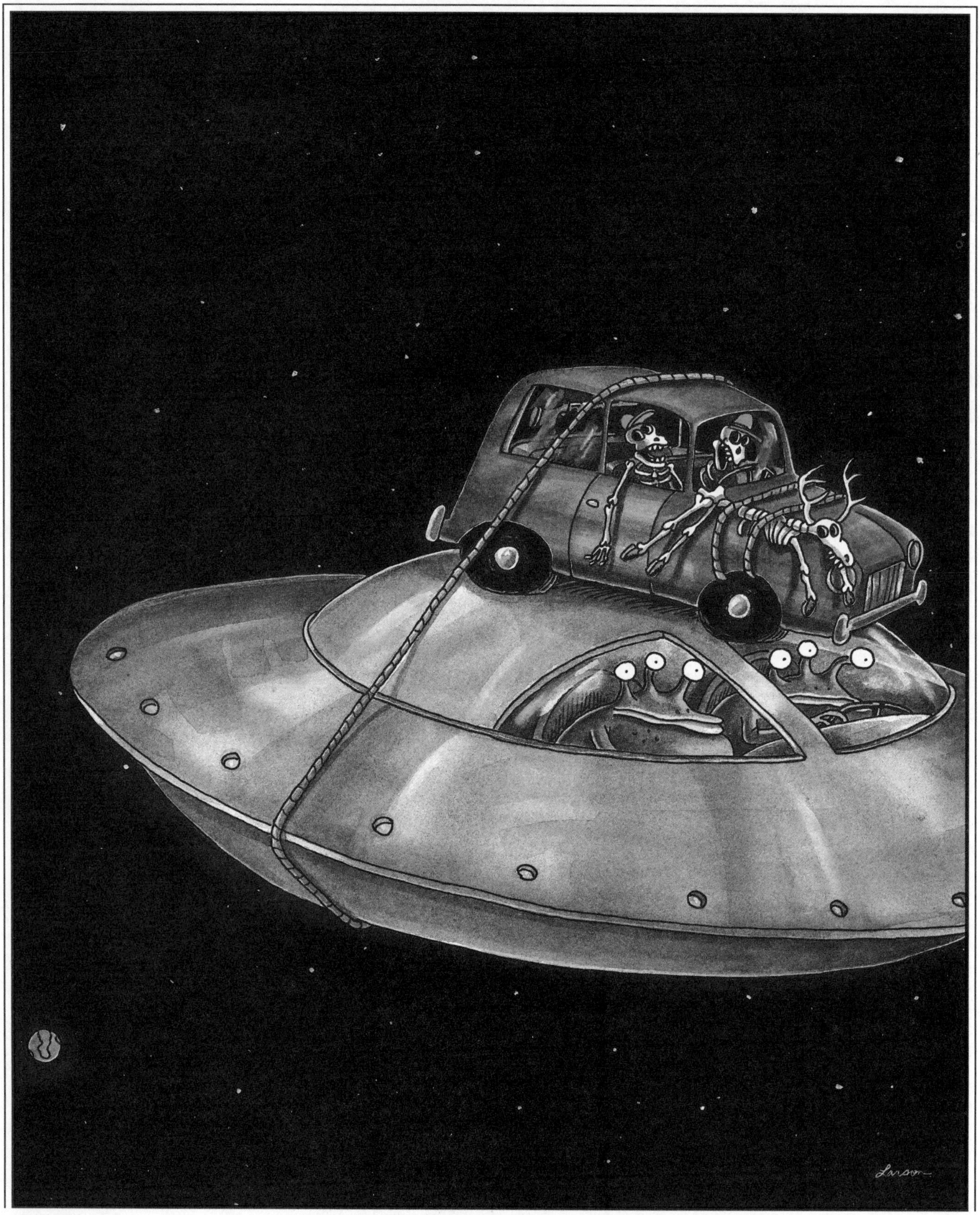
Larson

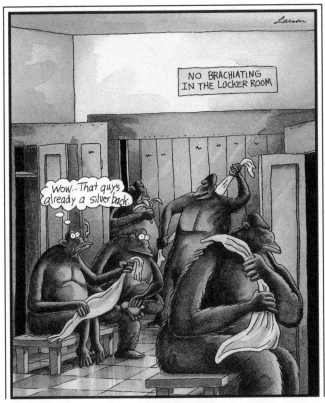

Junior high gorillas

How to recognize the moods of an Irish setter

"Look. We know *how* you did it—*how* is no longer the question. What we now want to know is *why*. ... Why now, brown cow?"

"Lord, we thank thee."

"So, they tell me you fancy yourself a tuba player."

The whole family always enjoyed the way
Uncle Numanga could reach over and "find"
a skull in little Tooby's ear.

"In this dramatic turn of events, testimony against
Mr. Pumpkineater is about to be given by his sister,
Jeannie Jeannie Eatszucchini."

The first Dirt Capades

"OK, McFadden. ... So *that's* the way you wanna play."

Eventually, Billy came to dread his father's lectures over all other forms of punishment.

"Well, here we are, my little chickadee."

Fly dates

Basic lives

The action suddenly stopped while both sides waited
patiently for the hornet to calm down.

"Curse you, Flannegan! Curse you to *hell*! ... There,
I've said it."

"Uh, let's see ... I'll try the mammoth."

Dance of the Beekeepers

At Electric Chair Operators Night School

"Give me a hand here, boys! It's young Will Hawkins!
... Dang fool tried to ride into the sunset!"

"Well, here he comes ... Mr. Never-Makes-a-Dud."

The life and times of baby Jessica

Every afternoon a sugar cube dealer would slowly
cruise the corral looking for "customers."

"Dogs that drink from the toilet bowl—after this."

Modern art critic

"Man, the Kellermans are bold! ... If it wasn't for our screens, they'd probably walk right in!"

"Oh, and *that* makes me feel even worse! ... I laughed at Dinkins when he said his new lenses were indestructible."

"OK, everyone just stand back! ... Anyone
see what happened here?"

"Same as the others, O'Neill. The flippers, the
fishbowl, the frog, the lights, the armor. ...
Just one question remains: Is this the
work of our guy, or a copycat?"

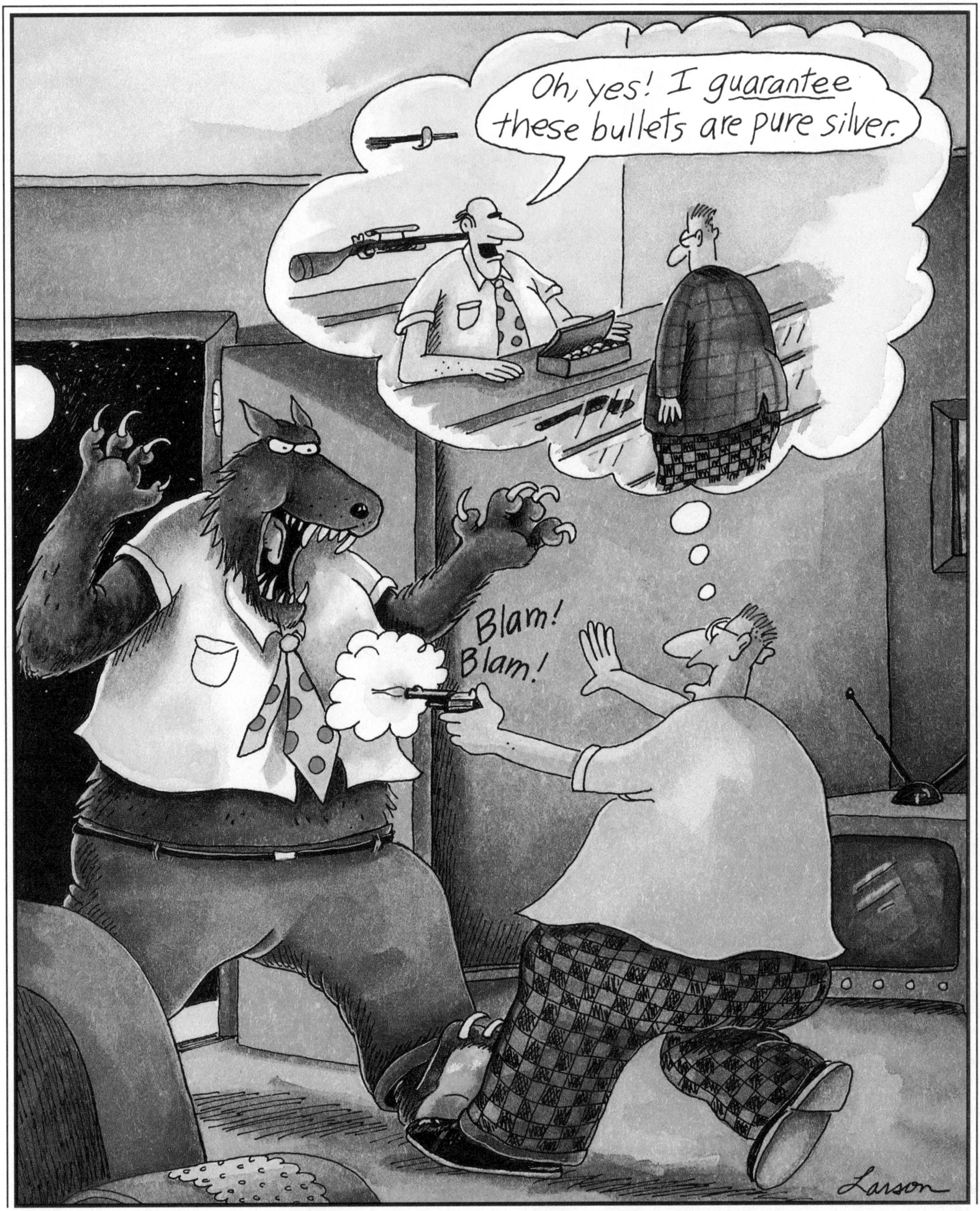
Oh, yes! I guarantee these bullets are pure silver.
Blam! Blam!
Larson

Moments before he was ripped to shreds, Edgar vaguely recalled having seen that same obnoxious tie earlier in the day.